Athina Klandt
Till I turn blue

About the book

This debut poetry collection is not only about coming
of age in our time and the struggles that accompany it.
This poetry questions you and this time. It gives you a
deep insight into the obsessive feelings of someone
who fell for the idea of someone. These words visualize
the void our mind can create. They show you the
absurdity of life.

Athina

Till I turn blue

Lyric poetry

Bibliografische Information der Deutschen
Nationalbibliothek: Die Deutsche Nationalbibliothek
verzeichnet diese Publikation in der Deutschen
Nationalbibliografie; detaillierte bibliografische Daten sind
im Internet über http://dnb.dnb.de abrufbar.

Verlag: BoD · Books on Demand GmbH, In de Tarpen 42,
22848 Norderstedt, bod@bod.de

Druck: Libri Plureos GmbH, Friedensallee 273, 22763
Hamburg

ISBN: 978-3-7693-0563-0

Till I turn blue I will write about you

Contents

The absurdity of life

Just a series of consequences

Humanity

We have lost our dreams.
Humanity divided into teams,
over too many countries.
Turned their backs on art.
Humanity lost its spark.
How are we better than animals,
when we torture and slaughter
for our own laughter?

10 Years

In 10 years,
you will have seen the future.
You will ask for more, and what for?
Remembering everything you once knew,
you will see, those lies were never the truth.

Your life wasn't gonna be yours.
You were never free to choose.
Your strength and precious youth,
it was all used,
everything, everyone abused,
for an economical growth use.

It's too late,
now you regret,
can't seem to forget.
Remorse tortures you to sleep.
Tears you involuntary weep.
In memory of your youthful you,
lighting a candle is all you can do.

"What a shame,
but don't complain",
that's all they always say.

A young poet

So many noises,
so many voices.
Why would you read my words?
Why would you listen to my voice?
I do not aspire.
I am not admired.
I don't know how to write.
I don't even properly rhyme.
I make use of the same old words.
My stupidity only hurts.
I write in a language,
I cannot call my mother tongue.
Hand me a bandage,
so my wounds won't stop me run.
So I don't slow down.
Cause soon I'm no longer young.
No longer beautiful or plump.
Then all you'll call me is dumb.

All those wasted lives

And they talk and talk about a tasteless world,
discussing its shades of white and black.
Describing the differences in their everyday, boring lives,
searching for a meaning in their meaningless demise.
Never trying to reach for a better, greater price.
They tell themselves that they are no longer in their prime.
But now at the end, at the finish line, I can only hear them
cry.
I hear them begging for another life in another lifetime.
I see them regretting in their last breaths.
Till death their bones were restless.

An emerald coloured mess

Here I am standing in my dark green dress.
Here I am, an emerald coloured mess.
After twelve years, it came to an end.
I knew for twelve years, 2024 will be it.
So how could I be so unprepared?
I knew for long when it will be the last of days.
But I am still stuck in the past.
It all happened too fast.
Now I must be all grown up.
But all I feel like is throwing up.
I am so, so scared.
Not that anybody really cares.
Time flies by,
no time to say a proper goodbye.

Back to strangers

It is weird to act like,
act like I don't know.
Like I don't care.
Like I don't know you.
Like you don't know me.
It is weird to act like strangers.
But it is everything except hard and maybe,
maybe it is because we became strangers.
But I can't help myself and ask myself all these unanswered,
unimportant questions.
Is your favourite colour still blue?
Or did you change it to red again?
How was your first birthday without me?
Are you happy now?
It is weird to act like strangers,
but it is even weirder to accept the fact that we became
strangers.

There are no words I could possibly say

Now I can see it.
I see how your pure, bright heart
got shattered and thrown into the dark.
Your dreams are only dreams
and you are not what you wanted to be.
It all fell apart
and you regret.
You have so much to regret.
There are so many tears you have shed.
You try to carry on,
as if nothing is going on.
You try to accept your everyday life,
it has you in a cycle of draining demise.
There are no words I could possibly say,
to take your lifelong agony and pain away.
You have done too much labour and tests,
your bones don't recognise the feeling of rest.
If I could,
I would take you to the beach.
There you would listen to the waves
and watch how the light plays silly little games.
I would give you a pencil and a world full of time,
so you could finally write.
Maybe then your eyes would regain their light.
If I could,
I would give you all the flowers in the world,
cause there is nobody who does more to deserve.

Grey eyes

I always thought you would achieve greatness,
but I've realised just now
that your head is empty
and the world caught you.
A normal life is all you'll do.
I see your future life,
stretching in your deep eyes.
They have lost their blue.
If only you knew,
that this grey,
is all that will stay.

I can hear the future

I like the way the music makes me feel.
I feel all my feelings so clear.
I no longer wish to disappear.
When I close my eyes,
I see a vision of myself
and I feel who I could be.
I see the future that could be achieved by me.
I feel the moments I could live,
if I only took the last step.

I see those empty fields.
I feel the wind carrying away my worries
and I feel Ideas floating into me.
Ideas and you believing in me.
How I wish to be there.

Crystal clear clarity

Crystal clear clarity
clashed into me,
when I saw a future,
I never wanted to see.
My mind doesn't fit
into this closed, narrow world,
which abandoned torturing words.
Abandoned true humanity,
in the need of pure luxury.
You are the only thing
to give me the needed oxytocin.

Play pretend

I think I dreamed of you.
But it was a different version of you.
He knew what to do.
He saw a beautiful life.
He thought it was worth the price.
This version was still my friend.
A friend who liked to play pretend.
A friend who crossed invisible lines.
A friend who made me feel scary lies.
In my dream we were a special kind of friends.
Friends who looked at each other one second too long.
Friends who know that something is really wrong.
Friends who ask themselves how it can feel so right
and who ask themselves when they have to pay the price.
Friends who just wait for their demise.
On the edge of breaking and collapsing,
the friendship keeps stretching,
in every possible direction.

Sixteen

The last days till I die, metaphorically.
Seventeen, the end I see.
In eleven days, an adult I'll be.
But why do I still feel like sixteen?
Will I then lose the ability to dream?
The ability to see?
See and feel what I need to be me?

I never really grew up.
At least that is what I tell myself.
But that is not quite right.
I've lived and learned.
I've lost and gained.
But an adult?
That can't be.
I am still sixteen.
One year ago was yesterday, I think.
I still feel like it is my first time to drink.
I still cannot give up.
I still am able to dream.
I hope I never lose what I knew,
when I was sixteen.

Smart boy

Tell me smart boy,
with those pretty eyes,
what is your sense in life?
Or will you live it in never ending demise?
Is it your family that keeps you alive?
Oh, you all are so alike.
Tell me,
did you ever think twice?
Did you ever dare to dream of what ifs?
Or did you just take the laid out path?
The path, where losing the direction,
could lead to your true passion?
Smart boy, start thinking twice.
You should stop following those lines.
Oh pretty boy,
I already see the end of your life,
in those light blue eyes.

Change

Something changed
and for the first time
I feel unable to put it in words.
Something changed.
I am not talking about my age
or being in my last week of school.
Something changed in me.
I am not talking about finally choosing,
choosing who is worth my time.
Something changed deep inside me,
while nothing changed at all.
Nobody can see or feel it,
but I feel it deep in my soul.
I feel like somebody.
I feel a deep, cold recognition.
I want a future.
I desire my dreams.
I feel that maybe I could be free.
I finally see beyond the horizon.
I finally caught some air.
I am finally breathing.
Breathing steady, calm breaths.
I am letting go.
I breathe in and out.
Something changed.
I changed
and maybe actually everything changed.

Something you can interpret how you want

The moon is shining,
he comes to live,
but for that
the sun first had to die.
´

The night swallowed her whole,
not that the moon would have ever asked for.
And the moon,
he has no choice but to raise
and now everything is in demise.

Everybody mourns after the day which is now past,
not praising the beautiful night which will never last.
All of you blinded,
not able to see
the beauty of something that won't always be.

But I will stay here praising
and romanticising the beauty.
Feeling the freedom of life,
the gift of the beautiful night.

Summer is dead

Summer does no longer feel like summer.
Even though I still crave my favourite Ice cream.
And even though I still got my same old friends.
And even though my world still seems to be okay.
And even though I still want to swim and drink,
everything is now different, I think.

Because now I care about the money I spend.
I see the price of my favourite Ice and I decline.
I still got my friends, but they have changed.
Everyone got different dreams to achieve.
Everyone got different places to be.
I still want to do those fun things we did,
but now it is different, I think.

I don't feel the adrenaline.
The exciting feeling of summer is gone.
The freedom of every day,
it holds me in a boring cage.
Don't know how to decide,
for a future that is only mine.
Who do I want to be?
I lost my sense in living.
I lost the passion that came with breathing.
I can no longer feel my heart beating,
because summer does no longer feel like summer.

Swaying

"Live in the moment",
they happily say,
but I just sway.

The waves crash me from my feet,
no holding point left to keep.
Time flows like a crashing river.
Drowning in his cold water, I shiver.
He can feel me quiver.

He never stops,
never slows down.
Can't find myself then nor now.
Past, present, future,
All unknown.

Sweet seventeen

Sweet seventeen,
still naive and full of dreams.
Desiring to be a poet and an artist.
Dreaming about the living.
Desiring to feel and write.
But I know this life won't always be right.
Under the pressure of daily life, I will crumble.
On my way to my future, I will stagger and stumble.
Dreams will be haunting me,
metamorphosing to nightmares.
A torturing desire, developed deep in my chest, won't be
rare.
There will be a time when I will feel lost and not slightly
okay.
But until then,
I'll be seventeen.

The cycle

It is a cycle we are in.
We lose and we win.
Lost my fantasy
and won my independency.

I was a little child
with wide, open, curious eyes.
I looked at the older
and saw how they got colder.

Feared for my future,
but admired the older.
Wishing to become beauty,
but I didn't see what they saw.

Now I'm older.
Now I see the little ones,
looking at me with these
wide, open, curious eyes.

Wishing to protect,
but that's not how you get older.
We lose and we win,
in this cycle we are stuck in.

Reflections

I see the world passing by,
in the reflection of my parents' eyes.
Feel their pain in this destructive world.
Their bodies tortured till final failure,
by a system you need to fit in,
a system that will never let you give in.
I see my future in their eyes.
Fear is rushing, streaming, pulsing through my veins.
A fear so real, a feeling I don't have to explain.
You can feel it too.
You see it in strangers' eyes.
You fear the day,
your eyes mirror theirs.

To a dying artist

Do you still play the guitar?
Or has life driven you too far?
Do you still paint?
Do you still skate?
Or did the cycle devour you?
Is now working all you do?
Do you chase the money like the rest?
Or are you still an artist, trying your best?
Do you still use English like it's your mother tongue?
Your talent—did you forget?

Autumn is coming back.
It reminds me of you.
It possesses me with questions.
Did you ban me from your mind?
Or do I occupy your time?
If you could say one last thing,
would you wish me the bling?
Or curse me endlessly?
All I want to say,
it could have ended differently.

True meaning

In the future, I will be a lawyer.
At least this is what my parents hope.
Oh no, I should better become a doctor.
Then I would be the pride of my family.
Or maybe they would be happier If I became an architect?
At least that's what everyone always told me.
"Study, get a rich man, get a good job, and make money.
Like everybody,
be like everybody, but better.
Have their dreams,
but be the one to accomplish them."

But nobody never asked me about mine.
I want to do something,
that gives my pathetic being a meaning.
Something money can't buy
and the richest man on earth can't get me.
I want to be an author and overcome death.
I want my words to change the world,
even when I've turned back to dirt.

Writing

The art of the lost ones.
The art of the hopeless romantics.
The art for those who feel like reading is not enough
and their minds and brains are too full.
Words bubbling in their liquid heads,
ready to flow down on paper.
The art for those who need to create their own worlds
in order to survive this world.
The art for those who cannot talk but have too much to tell.
The art for those who want their minds,
their heart and soul to overcome death.
The art for those who do not fear the depths of the unknown.

Writing.
The art of influencing and manipulating.
The art of obsession and romantic.
The art of the unspoken.

You moved on

Time went on,
but I never moved on.
Still living in two thousand twenty-one,
when your eyes filled me with passion
and my body gave you the earnest reaction.
The time I fell in love with a lie.
A time you still graced my eyes,
but now it is time to say goodbye.
We will no longer cross each other's lifes.
Time went on
and you moved on.

A series of consequences

I am not me.
I am not my body,
or the books I read.
I am not my mind,
or the things I write.

I am the consequence
of a series of random events.
I am made of my external conditions and environment.
I am made of the genes that gave me my shell.
I am made of the things people said to me.

I am everything and nothing.
I am just the consequence of all the things,
that triggered my senses.
I am just a series of consequences.

Obsession and Possession

It is always in the eyes

All your senses

Can you taste this?
This bittersweet spark?
The burning, hurting?
The sour shame?

Can you hear this?
My heart calling your name
and my mind screaming to stay sane.

Can you feel this?
My quickening breath on your arm
and the ghost of me lingering on your skin?

Can you smell this?
My perfume just for you
hoping that it will never let you go.

Can you see this?
Me searching for you behind
those dead, cold eyes.

Be mine

Don't trust your guilty mind.
Just turn around and be mine.
Don't worry, this may feel like a crime
but you know we don't have time.

Lock your eyes with mine.
I will let you drown,
I will let you suffocate,
I won't let you ever escape.

Don't turn your back on me.
You are already in too deep.
You know you would regret.
So just don't hold back.

Don't trust your guilty mind.
Just turn around and be mine.

The forbidden fruit

Something I can't have
and shouldn't even want.
Something that takes my breath away
and makes me want to stay
at a place I'm not meant for.
My mind and heart are torn.

The forbidden fruit, forbidden forever.
An all-time, forever-consuming muse,
evoking all of human's deepest curses.

Oh, how unbothered, unaware you are.
while I write all my poems about you.
I am cursed by you,
so, this is what I have to do.
Bond to my pen,
writing is all I can.

Do you?

Shiver down my spine.
Eyes look in mine.
Do you see me?
Do you still want me?

Or did you forget the unspoken?
Am I alone broken?
Cause I can't let go of your touch.
I know for you this wasn't much.

But every time I search your gaze,
I feel like you don't even recall my name.

Don't look away

I feel you looking.
I resist the urge.
I want to meet your gaze,
but you would escape.
So I let you stare.
Feel the heat,
let it creep.

I wish to capture you,
but in the end I never do.

I am your desire

Confess it.
Don't question it.
I know, don't worry.
Your vision is gonna be a little blurry.

I am the materialization of your desire,
the lost puzzle piece to complete.
I am everything you see.
There is nobody that could compete.
I am the one you desperately want to keep.
I am the one you desperately need.
Oh honey, I know what you seek.
If you want you can take the lead.

Just a fool

I would burn the world to see you shine.
Give my whole world to make you mine.
That's a fact I am unable to hide.
Wanna scream your name in the night.
You won't be able to close your eyes,
while my voice echoes through your mind.
I would do it all for you.
The small and the fatal disaster decisions.
Give you every piece,
would run every mile,
give you all my time.
Just a fool,
who turned into your tool.
Your love so limited,
of your presence I am intimidated.
Love so wrong, love so fake.
Love so one-sided, this can't be fate.
But I fell so hard, it's too late.
I will do it all for you.
Ruining me for you,
just so you don't have to.

Make him jealous

Look at me, so he feels you staring.
Jealousy shall be his constant companion,
because this tension is concerning.
Make him taste the bitterness of craving.
He shall see I am more than deserving.
So, stare at me,
I like your company.
Love to see what it will do to him.
I am more, so much more than deserving,
He shall be in a constant state of concerning.
Let me bath in your gaze,
it will vanish every hint of insecurity.
Let the tension take over,
I promise this won't have a consequence.

Still in my dreams

I dreamed about you.
It's been a long time since the last time.
Foolish me really thought,
this time I really thought,
that I've learned how to fly.
Fly far away from you.
But I never do.
You are still in my wings,
and your weigh is dragging me down.
You are still in those things,
you are still in my favourite colour.
You are embodying everything that's wrong.
How come I did not move on?
Why did I dream about you after so long?
But it does not matter, does it?
The dream will fade and you will never know,
that's how things always go.

Till the last day

The day will come
and we'll call it the last.
Time will simply pass.
Maybe in a couple of years I'll confess.
Don't think you'll be surprised.
Then, in a couple of years,
maybe you'll admit.
Admit to the fire I lit.
Admit the secrets you kept.
Maybe you'll play it off.
Maybe the game will never stop.

So play me like you always do.
I'll enjoy it as long as I can.
Because it will come.
Because the day will come
and we'll call it the last,
and a lot of time will pass.
Maybe we'll even forget.
But until then,
playing along is all I can.

Your touch

Sometimes I feel too much,
especially when I am allowed to feel your touch.
Every time I fall and fall way too deep.
Deep into emotions you wouldn't dare to ever understand.
Emotions your darkest dreams couldn't comprehend.
Emotions detached from any reasonability.
Emotions as raw as human cravings can be.
You are my weakness and my way.
You are the cause of my madness,
but as long as it is you, I will accept this endless.

Hells and heavens

And when I look in your eyes,
hells and heavens collide.
Violence on my mind.
Fights about rights and wrongs.
Wars over dos and don'ts.
Till my mind is not something I own.
Till my mind turns into an empty battlefield
and you are the only living being left to keep.
My mind, a slaughtered empty place,
with an exception that is yours to make.

Faded obsession

Suddenly, it happened.
It happened without a warning.
It wasn't a quiet, slow process,
but rather a loud crash,
right through my door.
One rainy, lonely night,
I realised that the desire was gone.
I did no longer feel.
I no longer felt desperate for you.
I no longer hungered after you.

Things I shouldn't feel

Why are we humans cursed to feel so deeply?

Autumn is in the air

I'm drained.
My mind,
always occupied by you.
Everything is spinning.
Don't know where to go.
Don't know what to feel.

The sky turned navy.
It got cold.
The music drumming
from my earphones
is stinging into my heart.
I think that's why I can't stop,
can't stop thinking about you.

"But it's not my fault",
I ensure myself.
There is something in the air
and in the way the leaves fall.
And how my shoes take their last breath.
And in the way the pouring rain hits my skin.

I'm sure autumn is in the air.
I'm sure it makes me feel those silly things.
I'm sure I'm just getting a bit nostalgic.
But I'm sure it's not about you.
I'm sure it's not about us
and how the pouring rain hit your skin,
or how you took the leaves's last breath.
I'm sure autumn is just in the air.

Thought I was over you

Thought I was over it.
Doesn't seem like it.
It took one look,
you got me hooked.
Your cursed silly smile,
it took me by surprise.
Those deep ocean eyes,
they lack life.
I searched their ground,
to find it all out.
Now I can't find my way out.
You feel me looking,
you play it off,
don't be a turn-off.
Play along
and don't you move on.
I know we have something in common.
Thought I was over you,
but that will never be true.

You always forget

You never remembered.
You always forgot
everything we shared.
How could you compare?
But I remember so vivid.
You were always so rigid.
I remember every shared moment.
I liked to act as your opponent.
Liked the challenges and the comparison.
It became a drug-like medicine.
Now I question if you ever cared,
of the answer I am scared.
This truth I'll never declare.
Cause you never remember,
you always forget.

Don't make me lie

Don't stare at me with those eyes.
I feel them pressing into my skin,
crawling under it and through it in.
Stop making me feel like this.
I do not want to be like this.
Don't make me search for more.
Don't make me lie, lie no more.
Lie to the moon.
Lie to the sun in the afternoon,
when I don't have anything to do.
Don't make me lie to my bedsheets.
Don't make me somebody I don't want to be.
Me, you shouldn't even see.
Take off your eyes.
Don't make me lie,
lie to myself.

Don't look behind

I want to give up.
Let you go,
at least not think about you.
I want someone to erase all my moments with you.
Maybe then I'll be free.
Maybe then I'll be able to see.
Seeing forward instead of only you behind me.
Don't you see?
I'm desperate and full of guilt.
So I'll drink and drink,
there is too much to think.
So I'll drink till I can't see.
Till I can't see straight forward me,
or left or right,
and definitely not behind.

The cold earth

"You are like fire,
so full of hate and love.
Full of fierceness and passion",
I used to say.
But no, that was never true.
You were always like the cold earth.
The fundament of life,
but so easy to despise.
Emotionless and lacking simple understanding.
Still, I desired a deeper connection.
You know, I mistook your emotionless dark,
for a fiery, mysterious spark.
Oh, what a fool I am.
You will never be the one to understand.

Forbidden yet inevitable words

Forbidden yet inevitable words,
even writing them hurts.
Want to hide the truth,
but not only from you.
Hiding from myself,
even those words won't help.
In the dark, my lies I craft,
but no shadow is deep enough.
The light is not far away.
One step from falling into despair.
Forbidden yet inevitable words,
even thinking them hurts.

Haunted

I saw you last night.
And the night before the night before.
What is it that you are here for?
Even after all those years,
it is you who rips me from sleep.
Oh, what could we have been?
I still see it in your eyes.
That summer, we should have been.
One summer to destroy my mind.
One summer, you should have been mine.
One summer, it should have been our time.
But we never got to be.
Now I'm left alone with what-ifs.
We never took the exciting risk.
We could have lived.
I'm haunted by moments we missed.
Haunted by a kiss,
which will never exist.

I beg you

I beg you to let your eyes,
let them wander across the room.
Let them stop when they finally see me.
Let them wander on my body, but slowly.
Let them take me in.
Let them take their time.

I beg you.
Let them make you lose focus.
Let them be trapped by me.
Let them see every detail.
Let them make my body burn.
I beg you to let them.
Let them define me.
Let them see something.
So, I can become something.

I remember all the things you forgot

I remember all the things you forgot.

I remember the things you wrote
and the lies you told.

I remember the way you looked at me
and how your hand touched my knee.

I remember your dirty little secrets
and how you told me to keep them.

I remember the way you promised me sweet nothings
and how you finally broke it.

I remember every little wink
and how it made my heart blink.

I remember the way you told me not to be scared
and how much I cared.

I remember you leaning over me
and how it made my heart skip two beats.

I still remember all the things you forgot.

Just a burden

I would turn my insides out
and hand them to you on a plate.
Just one word you have to say.
Give me the command
and I'll just jump.
I would do it all for you.
There is nothing I can't do,
when it comes to you.
But this unbalance I can't ignore.
I start to ask myself, "What for?",
when the simplest task
is the hardest burden to you.
When there is nothing you can do,
when it comes to me.

Just a fantasy

I feel these cold eyes,
shiver down my spine.
Or is it just my pride?
Maybe my mind doesn't function right.

Are you a fantasy
build by too much poetry?
Did I already lose my sanity?
You really make me question reality.

My mind plays a dangerous game,
just so it can feel the pain.
Because in the end, all we have is hate.

Just a game

Do you recall my name?
And the time you finally came?
I don't know how to explain,
but that felt like more than just a game.
What a shame,
but I can't complain.

Your fantasy gave me more,
than you could ever offer.
But still, I suffer.
Have you printed on my eyes.
Maybe it will get washed away.
But the feeling I crave,
it will stay.

What a shame,
I have to complain,
It's just a game.

Let her return

Did you take my love with you?
Tell me, what do I have to do?
Name your conditions for a return.
Let me go, and I'll tell you I've learned.
I'll tell you that I will stop falling so easily.
I'll promise not to mistake anyone for me.
I'll promise you this time, my love, I will keep.
I will keep her close to me.
So, nobody like you will ever steal.
I promise to finally treasure her.
I beg you, please, my love, let her return.

A tourist in my mind

Please leave my mind,
it's already been a long while.
You have wandered enough.
You have seen all of my wired mind
and even the deep parts I tried to hide.

But you still have not seen enough
and like a tourist,
you have left all your trash.
You are the reason this place will crash.
So, please leave my mind,
it's already been a long, long while.
There are new wanderers who should explore.
But you take up all the space.
You use it however you like,
while you pollute my mind.

Midnight questions

It is night.
The rain hits my window,
but not a single sign of sleep.
You are the reason, I believe.
I start asking myself,
what you are doing.
When was the last time,
your mind wandered in the wrong direction
and reminded you of my existence?
Did you even ever think of me?
Or did you lose every memory of me?
Is there nothing left to remind you?
Or do you simply not want to?
Am I even important enough to fill your mind?
Our lives are no longer intertwined.
I'm the night and left behind.
You are the day,
free from any despair.
You moved on.
You don't care.
And maybe I should do it like you.
I should stop wasting ink and paper,
stop destroying my confused mind.
You only ever cared about your reputation,
while I fell with no sight of salvation.

The non-existent

I wasn't even air to you,
cause then you would have needed me,
cause then I would have been something to you.

I was nothing to you.
I was non-existent to you,
while you were the one parasite deep in my gut.
Wouldn't let the non-existent go.
How could this imbalance exist?
Oh, how I craved a symbiosis.
I plead and begged to a god in my non-existence,
but the non-existence will never be heard.
And so I will be for the rest of my days,
the non-existent.

One last first kiss

All these feelings I shouldn't feel.
Feelings I shouldn't keep.
I am guilty.
I am dumb.
I wish to be numb,
so that the forbidden feelings vanish.
Them I want to banish.

Still, I want to feel you.
So, kiss me and let me fall.
Let this be the end, once and for all.
Let me move on.
Please, I beg, come on,
and grant me one last first kiss.

Paradox

I hate you.
I have all the reasons to.
You made me hate my favourite class.
You made everything about you.
You corrected me in every breath I took.
And you loved it, didn't you?
And you still love it with your whole, cold heart.
You love being better.
So much better than me.
So yeah, I should hate you.
Hate you like I hate dry hot days.
Like I hate the smell of vinegar.
Like I hate feeling small and dumb.
Like I hate being corrected.
Like I hate being worse than somebody else.
You are everything I hate
and yet, I can't bring myself to hate you.

Self-caused treason

Never enough.
I will never be enough.
Never be the one to be the best.
Never be the one to win the test.
Never be the one to make you put everything else to rest.
I am just too less.
Not worthy of your time,
not even of your mind.
How could I ever describe you,
when you are just as mesmerizing as the creation itself?
How could you ever choose me to waste your precious time?
Just let my lonely self rhyme and rhyme.
Occupy my mind and my mind.
Let my existence have a sense and a reason.
Let me stay in my self-caused treason.
I don't want to know about myself.
I am no longer somebody.
Not worthy of anything.
I'll stop talking and pleading.
So please let me spend my time,
with you on my mind.
Let my existence have a sense and a reason.
Let me stay in my self-caused treason.

You wouldn't understand

Since the book "Call me by your name"
one question is constantly running through my mind,
"Is it better to speak or to die?".
But you would never understand.
Why am I wasting my time?
I am the only one who is haunted.
By your presence I am taunted.
This one-sided relationship,
did you ever notice?
Did you ever see my pain?
Would you understand if I explain?
Oh, would you even care?
So I ask myself,
"Is it better to speak or to die?".

Till the end of all days

I see you when I don't want to,
when I can't help but long after you.
I see you when I close my eyes
and when I don't even try.
You give me sleepless nights
and a desire which makes me blind.
I see you all day.
When I try to and when I don't.
Maybe this feeling will stay,
cause I remember every sentence you got to tell.
You may or may not feel this way,
but I think you will haunt me till the end of all days.

Wicked smile

And when you left, I stopped,
stopped breathing and bleeding my brain on these innocent
pages.
Stopped making them filthy and stopped covering them in
agony.
Cause that is all you brought to me.
At least that is what I wish it to be.
But hope is agony's great accompaniment.
A combination that will be the reason for my downfall.
The reason I accuse myself of treason.
Cause this, I am not allowed to be feeling.
Now you found your way back in my weird, wired mind,
it took you not even a second of your time.
All you did was to give me that wide, wicked smile.

Till I turn blue

Till I turn blue,
I'll write about you.
Till the ocean runs dry,
you and I will deny.
Until skies tumble down,
in this feeling I will drown.
Drown deep into the unknown.
Drown deep into those ocean eyes.
I'll drown and drown in them,
till I turn blue.
That's when I can no longer write about you.

Your eyes had the same colour,
as the colour I was turning into.
It was all because of you.

The Void

In the void lies an enlightening hurtful truth

Academic validation

The pressure,
it is watching me.
Doing everything just to measure me.
Observing every little step I take.

It is chasing me.
Always right behind me.
Right on my neck.
Breathing right in my ear.
Goosebumps appear
and a shiver down my neck.
Is this a horror movie?

My heart cannot stop but race.
It takes too many turns in this maze.
It feels like being lost in a haze.
I fear losing my face.

My heart keeps running.
I do not fight the goosebumps nor the shiver.

So, I give it my best.
Just so I can pass.

Ain't I?

I am a disgrace.
Ain't I miserable?
Tell me, you all,
who wait for me to fall,
ain't I miserable?
Full of social anxiety,
which creeps inside of me.
I am shamefaced,
for my disgraced self.
Ain't I miserable?
So many words to use,
for my self-abuse.
Deplorable, detached,
whiny, wretched.
Oh, ain't I?

Beauty

I long for a beauty not a single soul can deny.
A beauty someone like you uses to write.
A body that is blessed by your heaven eyes.
A body that will pull you into hell's demise.
A beauty all throughout to my mind.
A beauty so deep in the soothing dark.
A beauty portrayed by statues in heaven's parks.
A beauty that makes you sell,
all your possessions, you don't even possess.
A beauty that will completely crumble the obsessed.

Decide

Time is running,
slipping through my fingers.
I try to scoop it from the ground,
but it is nowhere to be found.
Only seventeen,
I still have dreams to achieve.
But they force me to decide,
so I'll end up choosing not right.
Their eyes shine with dollar signs,
while I tell them I need more time.
Mother, you know how much I want to write.
I really want a fulfilled life.
I know I am good,
but will I be good enough?
Or should I give up?
Will I have enough time,
to evade my demise?

Derealization

The silence is too loud.
All I can see is unknown.
Please let me be normal again.
I can't feel like this again.
My room collapses.
It doesn't feel like mine.
Nothing belongs to me.
Nothing screams for me.
It feels like the void.
Nothing feels real.
Even these books lost their appeal.
I can't seem to see.
I want to scream.
But maybe,
maybe I should just sleep.

Doing it like you

The voices grew louder,
screamed at me to become quieter.
I try to whisper through to you,
but there is nothing I can do,
when you become as cold as ice.
My heart is the one who pays the price.
So, I just try to live a life in demise.
Blurry world, what a surprise.
You make me feel dumb,
like something you don't want.
You make me belittle myself.
You make me rip apart my face.
I feel like you never liked me,
and so I do it like you.
There is nothing I can do,
nothing to fix my face.
Instead, I can no longer stand myself.

Doubt

What am I fighting for,
when I can't see the horizon anymore?
I can't see the promised land
nor the dream of a loving hand.
I am no longer a teen,
now the harsh reality comes clashing in.

Nothing goes as planned.
It is going out of hand.
I try to read and write,
but how long do I have time?

Hate straight from hell

We are the object of their darkest and most disturbing
fantasies.
We are falsely embodied in every popular porno mainstream.
They hate us for the way we breathe
and for how we look and act.
But when their needs scream, they forget this fact.
They hate us talking back.
They want us to be scared dolls.
Just a silent, stupid toy.
A baby machine,
which keeps the house clean.
They'll say I'm exaggerating,
then how can you explain?
Men deciding over our bodies.
Don't you understand?
Deep down, society is the same.
No, not all men,
but most abusers are.
And with a given chance,
the number would be even higher.
It is not animalistic or desire,
that drives them to do such acts.
It is hate born straight from hell.

I'll just rhyme till the end of my time

I am bored of how I write.
There are too few words to describe.
I hate how I have to rhyme.
I just want to be seen.
Let me never die.
My words shall be there till the end of human time.
But where is the point,
I question myself,
when everything will vanish?
But what if we don't extinguish?
What if humankind finds a way not to die?
Would that make a difference?
I can't decide.
So, I'll just rhyme and rhyme,
while waiting for the end of my time.

Judgment day

If this was to end here,
what loss would be unable to bear?
If you could, on the last of all days,
if you could decide on judgment day,
who would fall
and who would rise,
would they finally pay their price?
And who would stay by your side?

No rescue

How can I speak about how I feel?
How can you comprehend and see,
when my mind is turning and turning.
It gets blurry on this journey.
No end in sight,
the start vanished in demise.
No going back.
Lost in this murdering mist,
without a rescuing plot twist.
This is it.
Can't recognize these constructs my mind creates.
I fall and fall,
losing it all.

Not paranoid

I always feel you in my dreams.
I always fall through one thousand seas.
I've seen the seven grounds.
I felt my body hitting bounds.
It was so calming cold.
Felt my limbs turning blue.
I swear what I say is true.
When I heard your voice,
took one last look at the void.
I am sure I am not paranoid.
Again, you won't push me down.
You will never let me drown.
I swear, I am sure!
I am sure that's what you've told me.
You pleaded and screamed, "Trust me",
and that's why I believe.
Paranoid? No need to be.

Right?

Metamorphosis

What can you do,
when there is no comfort you can turn to?
No security and no fundament.
Nobody for you to depend.
The common cycle stops.
Now you stand right before a dead end.
But as the doors open, you must choose.
Will you choose a path they will approve?
Or will you decide to stay to yourself true?
Will you follow through your plan?
Everything will change,
so why do you want to stay the same?
It's metamorphosis.
What will you do?
Your back you can't turn change to.

On the empty field

I feel so wrong,
so worn out.
My legs gave out.
They left me alone.
Just like you did.
Alone on the field.
The field you once filled,
filled with your laughter.
Now it feels like pure slaughter.
I am just somebody's daughter.
Spare my confused heart,
it got lost in the dark.
I don't want it to lose its last spark.
It shall find passion.
Passion unable for you to understand.
Unable for your species to comprehend.

Pullyourselftogether

My mind gets slaughtered and murdered.
Its ingr e die n ts   s   p   r e   a   d   al l o ver   th
e   pa p er.
Th e y   a s k   "What's the matter?".
They think to know it better.
They say I should pullmyselftogether.

Sometimes I don't feel human

Sometimes I don't feel human.
I don't understand the pleasure in dumb talking
and the sensation they get from mocking.
I see no point in running for my life,
it all seems so futile.
Why do we find ourselves in a circle,
for doing something that's insignificant?
These meals just waste my time,
trying hard to make up my mind.
Sometimes I am without any feelings to tame.
Pushing myself into the deep, dark void,
where my mind turns into a toy.
Playing games with itself,
without ever coming to an end.
Asking for the sense of life,
while I should be in my prime.
Sometimes all I feel is numbness,
mixed with a feeling of complete dumbness.
Unable to feel or see,
what is just wrong with me?
Sometimes I don't feel human.

Super silent violence

We battle in silence.
Super silent violence.
Acting like children.
Screaming in my mind.
Questioning my life.

Is it worth fighting?
Or should we keep the silence?
You don't know what to do.
I can't make up my mind.
Slowly wasting our time.

The parasite in my gut

I am so fucking dumb,
I wish to become numb.
So, I no longer want to bruise myself.
So, I no longer long to punch myself,
till I no longer feel my body,
till I feel like I am a nobody.
Rage fills my gut,
I want to see my blood.
Maybe then I'll calm down.
I want to smash my head against the wall.
Maybe then the parasite eating me up,
will finally come to a stop and give up.
But short before the finish line,
right before the win,
the parasite won't give in.
And at the end, there won't be something left to win.

Someone I once knew

The sound of falling leaves and the weeping wind.
I think it reminds me of you.
I think it sounds like the pain I once felt.
But who are you?
You, who is haunting me every time I go to bed.
You, who I do not remember.
I cannot recall the sound of your voice.
It faded away I believe,
like every part of you did.
And now, I do not remember.
Now, I cannot recall your face nor your eyes.
Were they brown or eventually blue?
I think they were blue.
A light blue almost white and cold like the sea you adored.
Or could they have been brown?
I think they were brown.
Brown like the fertile earth and the woods I admire.
I do not remember.
I cannot recall.
The faded memories haunt me in my unknown, blurred
dreams.
And I cannot recall the face nor the voice I once knew by
heart.
The face I recalled with my eyes closed
and the voice I recognized with my ears deaf.
Now a blurred face with no voice haunts me in my sleepless
nights.
And it might be you.
You, who I once knew.

The Walls

My mind is not able to comprehend.
Instead, the disturbance causes it to try to compensate.
The walls lose their sense.
They lose their structure and their colour.
What was my name again?
Who is this straight-staring figure,
eyeing me from the mirror?
My mind compensates by forgetting,
in this there is no regretting.
When everything is too much,
it makes me slowly lose touch.
I lose my face,
I lose my identity,
no chance for clemency.
It is too much sensation for my mind,
only one response to make everything right.
Banish my feelings and my existence,
left only with ugly panic and numbness.
The colourless walls stare at me in the darkness.

Unbecoming

You were in my dreams again.
Now I start to question everything again.
I tried to recall your voice.
It's slowly fading away.
I'm not sure if I'm happy or not.
Will I be free or not?
Will I long and be plagued by guilt?
Hard to move on,
from the person I built.
I still see your head tilt,
see your wink in my direction.
You were always my biggest distraction.
Every move you made gave you my reaction.
Let me lose your face and voice.
You shall become the void.

Vicious cycle

And while I wait and wait,
my mind spins and spins in a hazy pace.
It goes on, it does not stop to rotate.
It stumbles over its own creations.
Constructs of letters fill it to the brim.
I feel it getting dim.
It stretches in every direction,
every emotion ready for selection.
Everything could be happening,
while the reality looks so different.
Please answer and stop this vicious cycle.

Writer's block

The poets say, "With pain come the words".
But how come I lose the ability to form a word,
and how come I am unable to rhyme,
when I am at the lowest point of my life?
Why will creation only come at my prime?
Not allowed to pause because I'm running out of time.
I must continue to write,
to come forward in life.

Your soul

And if you could see your soul,
what would you see?
Would it be a bright light,
a warm glimpse that just feels right?
Or would it be the deep, dark sea?
No end in sight,
too many things it has to hide.
Is that how you would describe?
And would you call it "mine"?
Or did you lose it to another life?

Enlightening hurtful truth

Maybe, I think,
this defeating hit was not to avoid,
it had to happen.
It ripped me apart.
Leaving my poor heart in discard.
It made me bleed.
Now destructive words play on repeat.
But it had to be.
It was inevitable.
The hurtful truth
showed me what to do.
Destroyed the world as I view it.
Shattered me in a million pieces.
As they have fallen back into place,
I got a grasp of myself.
I realised,
I have never felt that right.
It is too hard to explain.
But for the first time in my life,
I got to realise,
what I must do.
I got to see,
what I want to be.
I got to feel,
what I never wanted to feel.
I now know what I desire.
I now know what I must obviate.
There is now no way for me,
to live in a constant state of compensation,
now that I grasped my meaning and desire.
There is now no way my dreams will ever retire.
I now know what I want from life.

I now know that it is mine.

To my love

You speak the language of my soul

Brown eyes

Eyes, oh deep blue eyes.
That's what they fantasize.
Their beauty I can't deny.
Felt it shattering my heart,
felt them tearing my mind apart.
Oh, deep blue eyes,
My tragic, tragic demise.
Oh brown, brown eyes,
My rescuing price.
Fixing my mind
through simple stitching,
feeling my heart twitching.
From them I don't want to hide.
Better than those deep blue eyes,
who never tried to hide their nasty pride.

Anticipation

Anticipation is killing me.
The day I finally want to see.
All those pure, hopeful hopes,
I hope will not be destroyed.
The day I planned for months.
Don't turn me upside down.
Don't leave my stomach empty
and my heart hungry for more.
Fill it with dazzling beauty.
Fill it with unforgettable memories.
Give me stories I will be able to tell.
Let me feel alive,
please fill my life with a surprise.

Afraid

Constant self-sabotage.
Constant self-doubting.
Afraid of being replaced.
Afraid that you see what they see.
Afraid that the cycle repeats.
Afraid it will never be me.
Afraid of silver medal, second place.
This cycle, it just rotates.
Everybody better than me,
afraid that you might see.

A reddish grey

You said you would give me the world,
just for me to give you a return.
I am the one who hurt the saint,
the one who destroyed your colourful paint.
Now there is only a reddish grey
and a red shade is already fading away.
I should set you free,
too numb to feel
your warmth.
Still, I feel the salty burn
combined with this annoying blur.
You deserve the moon and the stars,
while I should watch you from afar.

I am tainted

I want to give you the sweet love,
the love you dream of.
The love you deserve.
The love that gives you comfort.
And I'll try my best,
my best to pass this love test.
I'll put on a sweet scent,
which will blur your mind.
But be careful because time
will show my tainted, carved heart,
full of craving, longing desire.
It longs to never tire.
It longs to lock you away,
from this world full of despair.
Make you only mine.
Nobody will take your time.
There is no moving on.
In this, we'll stay.
Even death shall not do us apart.
There will be no leaving,
just don't forget about breathing.

The art of noticing

Noticing the little details,
the little, important details.
They shape my eyes.
Noticing the one hair,
that seems to rebel.
Noticing the clothes you choose
and how your body moves.
It's impossible to not notice
the beauty you hold,
when you act so bold.
The art of noticing,
something I'm great at.
You my muse,
left me no choice but
to become an artist in noticing.

The other half

The sky is empty.
No lonely clouds in sight.
An oppressive blue,
fills the endless void.
I miss you.
My soul aches.
It counts and counts
the endless seconds,
till reunion with its other half.
So it will be understood again,
so it can speak without explanation.
It waits and waits,
so it can again communicate.

The sound of my soul

My head is empty.
I don't know what to feel.
I don't even feel real.
I listen to the ocean,
clashing right into my heart.
I listen to the rain,
turning into one with the ocean,
and I try to hear myself in it.
I can't decipher it.
I can't distinguish it.
Oh tell me,
do you know what my soul sounds like?
Can you play your song for me?
So I can find myself in yours.

Why did you choose me?

I can see myself as the worst.
The bad, bad guy.
The one to despise.
So, stop telling me lies.

How I wish to see through your eyes.
Maybe you would convince me that I am good.
Maybe then I could see why I am the one you took.
I have no words for my shameful self.
I wish to only use them for you.
That way they have a sense,
that way I can say what I meant.
Full of beauty and bewitching compositions,
just for you.
Words I want you to turn to.
Words to show your beautiful self through my unworthy
eyes.
How could you ever grace me with the word "mine".
I am someone you should despise.

You are always there

While I was losing my mind,
you showed me I still had time.
You told me you would remember my name.
You showed me how to stay sane.

Craving you

How you grace the piano with your elegant fingers,
I can't resist but let my longing eyes linger.
I feel weird emotional waves deep in my gut.
I hope to be graced by your touch.
I crave your tender touch.
Sometimes it just feels like it's too much.
But I don't dare to take my eyes off you,
scared of missing a simple sound slipping from your fingers.
I can't help but let this moment linger.
I crave you like crazy.
I feel mad and hazy.
I want to become yours,
so you can be mine.
Give me all of your time.
Grace me with your touch while I cry.
You know, sometimes it is just too much.

Forever

Even in my darkest nightmares,
in which your ghost haunts
and tortures me,
I will call your name.
Even your darkest sides will forever be my light.
And even when you've lost your mind,
I will be right by your side.
And if you ever want to die,
I will be the one to bring you back to life.

The absurdity of life
Obsession and Possession
Things I shouldn't feel
The void
To my love

I was desperate and *possessed*,
for four years you were my only request.
But my whole life I never aced your test.
My whole life I had to question,
"What is the difference between *love* and *obsession*?"
But you never answered.
I fell deep into *the void*.
There I only imagined your voice.
I realised *the absurdity of life,*
with sixteen I felt the price.
On your command I would kneel,
but that was never to your appeal.
I felt *things I should never feel*.
It felt like drowning.
I saw my hands turning blue,
saw my vision turning blurry too.
Breathing and thinking became hard.
Then I saw his spark.

All I saw was you
and you answered my question.
I finally felt passion.
To my love,
there is nothing I wouldn't do for you,
because I am still made out of obsession.
Now you are my greatest *possession*.

I will write about you,
till I turn blue.

Afterword

Turning blue has three different meanings.

In my first one-sided and non-existent relationship with a boy it meant to drown in the unknown and in the words my mind created. I drowned in the things I wished and imagined. I drowned in his eyes and in the idea of him. I was delusional to the point where I lost my sense of reality. I was turning blue.

Secondly, it means to drown in distress or in a feeling of loneliness and hopelessness. It means drowning in the endless void that my mind created.

Lastly, turning blue refers to me drowning in my strong feelings. I drown in feelings and words till I lose myself. Till the feeling is so thick and strong that I am unable to talk about it. I drown.

I turn blue, unable to keep writing.

-Athina

About the author

I was born in 2006 in Germany, not that this is of any matter. For all of you, I go by the name "Athina". Like so many others, I love writing and reading. I write poems concerning obsession, coming of age, the absurdity of live, and feminism.

I am just a stranger, but I could be a stranger you know of.

Instagram: @athina_cak

Tiktok: @athina_cak